Starter: 150 vocabulary words

Tian Ji and the Horse Racing

田忌赛马

许晓华 改编

MP3 Download Online
www.sinolingua.com.cn

First Edition   2016

ISBN 978-7-5138-1017-3
Copyright 2016 by Sinolingua Co., Ltd
Published by Sinolingua Co., Ltd
24 Baiwanzhuang Road, Beijing 100037, China
Tel: (86) 10-68320585 68997826
Fax: (86) 10-68997826 68326333
http://www.sinolingua.com.cn
E-mail: hyjx@sinolingua.com.cn
Facebook: www.facebook.com/sinolingua
Printed by Beijing Jinghua Hucais Printing Co., Ltd

Printed in the People's Republic of China

编者的话

对于广大汉语学习者来说，要想快速提高汉语水平，扩大阅读量是很有必要的。"彩虹桥"汉语分级读物为汉语学习者提供了一系列有趣、有用的汉语阅读材料。本系列读物按照词汇量进行分级，并通过精彩的故事叙述，给读者带来了丰富有趣的阅读享受。本套读物主要有以下特点：

一、**分级精准，循序渐进**。我们参考了新汉语水平考试（HSK）词汇表（2012年修订版）、《汉语国际教育用音节汉字词汇等级划分（国家标准）》和《常用汉语1500高频词语表》等词汇分级标准，结合《欧洲语言教学与评估框架性共同标准》（CEFR），设计了一套适合汉语学习者的"彩虹桥"词汇分级标准。本系列读物分为7个级别（入门级*、1级、2级、3级、4级、5级、6级），供不同水平的汉语学习者选择，每个级别故事的生词数量不超过本级别对应词汇量的20%。随着级别的升高，故事的篇幅逐渐加长。本系列读物与HSK、CEFR的对应级别，各级词汇量以及每本书的字数详见下表。

---

* 入门级（Starter）在封底用S标识。

级别	入门级	1级	2级	3级	4级	5级	6级
对应级别	HSK1 CEFR A1	HSK1-2 CEFR A1-A2	HSK2-3 CEFR A2-B1	HSK3 CEFR A2-B1	HSK3-4 CEFR B1	HSK4 CEFR B1-B2	HSK5 CEFR B2-C1
词汇量	150	300	500	750	1 000	1 500	2 500
字数	1 000	2 500	5 000	7 500	10 000	15 000	25 000

二、**故事精彩，题材多样**。本套读物选材的标准就是"精彩"，所选的故事要么曲折离奇，要么感人至深，对读者构成奇妙的吸引力。选题广泛取材于中国的神话传说、民间故事、文学名著、名人传记和历史故事等，让汉语学习者在阅读中潜移默化地了解中国的文化和历史。

三、**结构合理，实用性强**。"彩虹桥"系列读物的每一本书中，除了中文故事正文之外，都配有主要人物的中英文介绍、生词英文注释及例句、故事正文的英文翻译、练习题以及生词表，方便读者阅读和理解故事内容，提升汉语阅读能力。练习题主要采用客观题，题型多样，难度适中，并附有参考答案，既可供汉语教师在课堂上教学使用，又可供汉语学习者进行自我水平检测。

如果您对本系列读物有什么想法，比如推荐精彩故事、提出改进意见等，请发邮件到 liuxiaolin@sinolingua.com.cn，与我们交流探讨。也可以关注我们的微信公众号 CHQRainbowBridge，随时与我们交流互动。同时，微信公众号会不定期发布有关"彩虹桥"的出版信息，以及汉语阅读、中国文化小知识等。

韩 颖 刘小琳

Preface

For students who study Chinese as a foreign language, it's crucial for them to enlarge the scope of their reading to improve their comprehension skills. The "Rainbow Bridge" Graded Chinese Reader series is designed to provide a collection of interesting and useful Chinese reading materials. This series grades each volume by its vocabulary level and brings the learners into every scene through vivid storytelling. The series has the following features:

I. A gradual approach by grading the volumes based on vocabulary levels. We have consulted the New HSK Vocabulary (2012 Revised Edition), the *Graded Chinese Syllables, Characters and Words for the Application of Teaching Chinese to the Speakers of Other Languages (National Standard)* and the 1500 Commonly Used High Frequency Chinese Vocabulary, along with the Common European Framework of Reference for Languages (CEFR) to design the "Rainbow Bridge" vocabulary grading standard. The series is divided into seven levels (Starter*, Level 1, Level 2, Level 3, Level 4, Level 5 and Level 6) for students at different stages in their Chinese education to choose from. For each level, new words are no more than 20% of the vocabulary amount as specified in the corresponding HSK and CEFR levels.

---

* Represented by "S" on the back cover.

As the levels progress, the passage length will in turn increase. The following table indicates the corresponding "Rainbow Bridge" level, HSK and CEFR levels, the vocabulary amount, and number of characters.

Level	Starter	1	2	3	4	5	6
HSK/ CEFR Level	HSK1 CEFR A1	HSK1-2 CEFR A1-A2	HSK2-3 CEFR A2-B1	HSK3 CEFR A2-B1	HSK3-4 CEFR B1	HSK4 CEFR B1-B2	HSK5 CEFR B2-C1
Vocabulary	150	300	500	750	1000	1500	2500
Characters	1000	2500	5000	7500	10,000	15,000	25,000

II. Intriguing stories on various themes. The series features engaging stories known for their twists and turns as well as deeply touching plots. The readers will find it a joyful experience to read the stories. The topics are selected from Chinese mythology, legends, folklore, literary classics, biographies of renowned people and historical tales. Such widely ranged topics would exert an invisible, yet formative, influence on readers' understanding of Chinese culture and history.

III. Reasonably structured and easy to use. For each volume of the "Rainbow Bridge" series, apart from a Chinese story, we also provide an introduction to the main characters in Chinese and English, new words with English explanations and sample sentences, and an English translation of the story, followed by comprehension exercises and a vocabulary list to help users read and understand the story and improve their Chinese reading skills. The exercises are mainly presented as objective questions that take on various forms with moderate difficulty. Moreover, keys to the exercises are also provided. The series can be used by teachers in class or by students for self-study.

If you have any questions, comments or suggestions about the series, please email us at liuxiaolin@sinolingua.com.cn. You can also exchange ideas with us via our WeChat account: CHQRainbowBridge. This account will provide updates on the series along with Chinese reading materials and cultural tips.

Han Ying and Liu Xiaolin

主要人物和地点
Main Characters and Places

齐　王 (Qí Wáng)：齐国的国王。他喜欢赛马，有很多好马。

King of Qi: The king of the State of Qi (C1100 BC—221 BC). He loved horse racing and had many fine horses.

田　忌 (Tián Jì)：齐国的大将。他也喜欢赛马。

Tian Ji: A general of the State of Qi. He loved horse racing, too.

孙　膑 (Sūn Bìn)：田忌的朋友。他是一个很聪明的人。

Sun Bin: A friend of Tian Ji. He was a very intelligent man.

齐　国 (Qíguó)：中国古代的一个诸侯国。

State of Qi: A state in ancient China.

中文故事

田忌赛①马②

① 赛 (sài) v. race
e.g., 他喜欢看赛马。

② 马 (mǎ) n. horse
e.g., 我喜欢马。

③ 大将 (dàjiàng) n. general
e.g., 他是大将,有很多好马。

④ 常常 (chángcháng) adv. often
e.g., 我常常去朋友家。

齐国有很多人喜欢赛马,齐王喜欢,齐国大将③田忌也喜欢。他常常④和齐王一起赛马。

田忌和齐王都有三种①马——上马、中马和下马。上马是最好的马，下马是最不好的马，中马是一般②的马。

① 种 (zhǒng) *m.w.* kind, type
e.g., 这种水果叫什么？

② 一般 (yìbān) *adj.* general, ordinary
e.g., 星期天的下午，你一般做什么？

① 通常 (tōngcháng)
adv. normally, usually
e.g., 吃完晚饭，我通常会去散步。

② 比赛 (bǐsài)
v. have a match
e.g., 我想去参加跑步比赛。

③ 场 (chǎng) m.w.
round
e.g., 我们去看了一场电影。

赛马的时候，人们通常①会用上马和上马比赛②，中马和中马比赛，下马和下马比赛。一共三场③比赛。

齐王的每一种马都比田忌的好，所以每次比赛，齐王都赢①。

① 赢 (yíng) v. win
e.g., 我赢了这场比赛，我很高兴。

① 输 (shū) v. lose
e.g., 那场比赛，他输了，他很不高兴。

因为每次赛马都输①，田忌很不高兴，他不想和齐王赛马了。

有一天,齐王说:"田忌,今天① 你和我赛马,好吗?"田忌说:"对不起,我今天身体不好,不能赛马。"

① 今天 (jīntiān)
n. today
e.g., 今天,我要去看一个朋友。

① 明天 (míngtiān)
n. tomorrow
e.g., 明天, 你去哪儿?

② 吧 (ba) part. (used at the end of imperative sentences to soften the tone)
e.g., 这个房间很好, 你看看吧。

③ 办法 (bànfǎ)
n. solution
e.g., 你有什么办法?

齐王说:"那明天①吧②。"田忌没有办法③, 说:"好吧, 明天。"田忌回家了。可是, 那天他不太高兴。

家人问他,为什么不高兴。田忌说:"齐王想和我赛马,可是我不想和他赛马。因为,他的马比我的马好,我一定会输。"

① 告诉 (gàosu)
v. tell
e.g., 他告诉我，他想回家。

家人听了，也没有办法。这时候，他的朋友孙膑来了。孙膑也问他为什么不高兴。田忌就把赛马的事告诉①了他。

孙膑也喜欢赛马，他听了，笑着说："我有一个好办法。你去和齐王赛马吧，这次你听我的，一定会赢。"田忌问："真的？"

孙膑说:"当然是真的。"田忌问:"你有好马,想给我?"孙膑说:"我没有好马。"田忌说:"没有好马,我一定还会输!我真不想去了!"

孙膑笑了，说："你听我的，去吧。没问题！"田忌说："快告诉我，是什么好办法！"孙膑就把他的办法告诉了田忌。

① 聪明 (cōngmíng)
adj. smart, intelligent
e.g., 他很聪明。

听了朋友的办法，田忌也笑了，说："你真聪明①！"他觉得孙膑的办法真的很好！

第①二天,齐王来了,田忌和孙膑也来了。齐王觉得自己能赢,高高兴兴的。

① 第 (dì) *prefix.* (marker of ordinals) e.g., 今天是比赛的第一天。

田忌也觉得自己能赢,也高高兴兴的。

齐王看着田忌,说:"你看看我的马,再① 看看你的马。你觉得今天你能赢吗?"田忌说:"当然能赢。"

① 再 (zài) *adv.* (used to indicate the occurrence of an action after another) then e.g., 我要把这本书看完再走。

① 开始 (kāishǐ)
v. begin
e.g., 比赛什么时候开始?

赛马开始①了。第一场比赛,<u>田忌</u>用下马和<u>齐王</u>的上马比赛。

田忌输了,但是他没有不高兴。齐王赢了,当然很高兴。

第二场比赛,田忌用上马和齐王的中马比赛。田忌赢了,他笑了。

齐王有点儿不高兴了。可是他想，还有第三场比赛呢①。

① 呢 (ne) *part.* (used at the end of declaratives to stress a fact and make a convincing case)
e.g., 妈妈，哥哥不在，还有我呢。

第三场比赛,田忌用中马和齐王的下马比赛,田忌又赢了。田忌很高兴,但是齐王很不高兴。

比赛结果①,田忌赢了两场,输了一场,2:1赢了齐王。齐王说:"今天赛马,你的办法太好了。"

① 结果 (jiéguǒ)
n. result
e.g., 我想知道今天的比赛结果。

田忌说:"这个办法是孙膑告诉我的。"齐王问:"孙膑是谁?他在哪儿?"田忌说:"他是我的朋友,今天也来了。"

齐王觉得孙膑很聪明,想见见他。见面以后,他很喜欢孙膑,就让他做了齐国的大将。

> **English Version**

Tian Ji and the Horse Racing

Many people in the State of Qi loved horse racing. The King of Qi loved it like many of his subjects, so did Tian Ji, a general of Qi. He often raced horses with the king.

Both Tian and the king had three types of horses, specifically, superior, average, and inferior ones. Superior horses were the best horses, inferior were the slowest, and average were just mediocre horses.

During the horse races, a superior horse would normally compete against another superior horse, an average against another average, and an inferior against another inferior. There were three rounds in total per match.

Each of the king's horses was better than Tian's. As a result, the king won every time.

Since Tian lost every match, he was unhappy. He didn't want to race horses with the king anymore.

One day, the king suggested, "Tian, would you like to race horses with me?" Tian replied, "Sorry, I am not feeling well so I can't race horses today."

The king responded, "Then how about tomorrow?" Tian had no choice but to say yes. Tian went home; however, he was not happy at all.

His family asked him why he was upset. Tian answered, "The king wants to race horses with me, but I don't want to because his horses are better than mine. I am doomed to lose."

His family couldn't think of any solution to help him. Then his friend Sun Bin dropped by. Sun asked why he was unhappy. Tian told him about the king and horse racing.

Sun also loved racing horses. Hearing that, he said with a smile, "I have a good solution. Go ahead and race the king. Follow my advice and you will surely win." Tian doubted his friend and said, "Really?"

Sun replied, "Of course." "Are you giving me your fine horses?" asked Tian. Sun replied, "I don't have any fine horses." "Without fine horses, I will definitely lose again! I really don't want to go," argued Tian.

Sun smiled and reassured his uneasy friend, "Just trust me and go. Everything would be fine." Tian urged, "Come on, tell me what your strategy is!" Sun told Tian his plan.

After hearing his friend's plan, Tian smiled and said, "You are so smart!" He thought his friend's plan was really good!

The following day, everyone arrived at the races. The king seemed very happy because he was so confident.

Tian thought he could win now so he was also in good mood.

The king looked at Tian and said, "Look at my horses, then look at yours. Do you think you have any chance to win today?" "I sure do," answered Tian.

The horse race began. For the first round, Tian used his inferior horse to race against the king's superior horse.

Tian lost that round, but he was not upset. The king won and was very happy.

The second round, Tian used his superior to beat the king's average. Tian won and smiled.

The king was a little unhappy, but he remained confident for the third round.

The third round, Tian used his average horse to race against the king's inferior horse. Tian won again! Tian was very happy while the king was very unhappy.

The final result of the race: Tian won two rounds and lost one, beating the king 2:1. The king praised his general and said, "Your strategy was marvelous in today's race."

Tian explained, "It was Sun Bin who told me this solution." The king asked, "Who is Sun? Where is he?" Tian said, "He is my friend and is also here today."

The king thought Sun was very smart and wanted to meet him. Upon meeting him, he appreciated Sun very much and thus appointed him general of Qi.

课前练习 Warm-up exercises

一、朗读下面的短语。Read the following phrases.

xǐhuan sàimǎ 喜欢赛马　yì chǎng bǐsài 一场比赛　gāogāoxìngxìng 高高兴兴

yídìng huì shū 一定会输　dāngrán néng yíng 当然能赢

二、思考题。Pre-reading questions.

1. 为什么以前赛马的时候，齐王都赢了田忌？

2. 这一次赛马，孙膑有什么好办法？

课后练习 Reading exercises

一、阅读故事，完成问题。Read the story and answer the following questions.

1. 故事中有三个人物，他们是齐王、_____和孙膑。

2. 按照正确的顺序排列下面的句子。

   A. 田忌赢了。

   B. 田忌不高兴。

   C. 每次赛马比赛，齐王都赢，田忌都输。

   D. 孙膑做大将。

   E. 孙膑有一个办法。

   （1）____ （2）____ （3）____ （4）____ （5）____

二、为下列各题选择正确的答案。 Choose the correct answer according to the story.

1. 田忌和齐王赛马，有（　　）比赛。

   A. 一场　　B. 二场　　C. 三场　　D. 很多

2. 以前，田忌和齐王赛马的办法是（　　）。

   A. 上马 vs 上马　　　　B. 上马 vs 中马

   C. 上马 vs 下马　　　　D. 中马 vs 下马

3. 今天，田忌的下马和齐王的（　　）马比赛。

　　A. 上马　　　B. 中马　　C. 下马

4. 今天，田忌的中马和齐王的（　　）马比赛。

　　A. 上马　　　B. 中马　　C. 下马

5. 田忌和齐王的比赛结果是（　　　）。

　　A. 1:2　　　B. 2:1　　　C. 3:0　　　D. 0:3

> **三、判断题：请根据故事内容判断下列说法是否正确，如果正确请标"T"，不正确请标"F"。**
> **Decide whether the following statements are true (T) or false (F).**

1. 在齐国，有很多人喜欢赛马。　　　　　　（　　）
2. 齐王的马比田忌的马好。　　　　　　　　（　　）
3. 田忌不喜欢齐王，所以不想赛马了。　　　（　　）
4. 孙膑想给田忌一些好马。　　　　　　　　（　　）
5. 用了孙膑的办法，田忌赢了。　　　　　　（　　）

四、看图复述故事内容。Fill in the blanks to retell the story using the pictures.

1. _____的马都比_____的好，所以每次比赛，齐王_____。

2. 田忌说："我_____和他赛马。因为，他的马比我的马好，我_____。"

3. 孙膑笑着说："我有_____。你去和齐王赛马吧，这次你_____。"

4. 比赛结果，田忌_____两场，_____一场，_____赢了齐王。

5. 田忌说:"这个办法是孙膑_____的。"齐王问:"孙膑_____?他在_____?"

课后练习答案 Keys to the exercises

一、阅读故事，完成问题
1. 田忌
2.（1）C （2）B （3）E （4）A （5）D

二、为下列各题选择正确的答案
1. C　2. A　3. A
4. C　5. B

三、判断题：请根据故事内容判断下列说法是否正确，如果正确请标"T"，不正确请标"F"
1. T　2. T　3. F　4. F　5. T

四、看图复述故事内容
1. 齐王　田忌　都赢
2. 不想　一定会输
3. 一个好办法　一定能赢
4. 赢了　输了　2:1
5. 告诉我　是谁　哪儿

词汇表
Vocabulary List

吧	part.	ba	(used at the end of imperative sentences to soften the tone)
办法	n.	bànfǎ	solution
比赛	v.	bǐsài	have a match
常常	adv.	chángcháng	often
场	m.w.	chǎng	round
聪明	adj.	cōngmíng	smart, intelligent
大将	n.	dàjiàng	general
第	prefix.	dì	(marker of ordinals)
告诉	v.	gàosu	tell
结果	n.	jiéguǒ	result
今天	n.	jīntiān	today
开始	v.	kāishǐ	begin
马	n.	mǎ	horse
明天	n.	míngtiān	tomorrow
呢	part.	ne	(used at the end of declaratives to stress a fact and make a convincing case)
赛	v.	sài	race
输	v.	shū	lose
通常	adv.	tōngcháng	normally, usually
一般	adj.	yìbān	general, ordinary
赢	v.	yíng	win
再	adv.	zài	(used to indicate the occurrence of an action after another) then
种	m.w.	zhǒng	kind, type

项目策划：韩　颖　刘小琳
责任编辑：韩　颖　彭　博
英文编辑：范逊敏
英文翻译：潘婉雯
封面设计：E·T创意工作室

图书在版编目（CIP）数据

田忌赛马：汉、英 / 许晓华改编． — 北京：华语教学出版社，2016
（"彩虹桥"汉语分级读物．入门级：150词）
ISBN 978-7-5138-1017-3

Ⅰ．①田… Ⅱ．①许… Ⅲ．①汉语－对外汉语教学－语言读物 Ⅳ．①H195.5

中国版本图书馆CIP数据核字（2015）第230160号

田忌赛马
许晓华　改编

*

©华语教学出版社有限责任公司
华语教学出版社有限责任公司出版
（中国北京百万庄大街24号　邮政编码 100037）
电话：(86)10-68320585　68997826
传真：(86)10-68997826　68326333
网址：www.sinolingua.com.cn
电子信箱：hyjx@sinolingua.com.cn
新浪微博地址：http://weibo.com/sinolinguavip
北京京华虎彩印刷有限公司印刷
2016年（32开）第1版
2016年第1版第1次印刷
（汉英）
ISBN 978-7-5138-1017-3
定价：15.00元